DAILY

2020

(January 2020 - December 2020)

👤 _____

✉ _____

📞 _____

2020

Twenty twenty

January

S	M	T	W	T	F	S
			1	2	3	4
5	6	7	8	9	10	11
12	13	14	15	16	17	18
19	20	21	22	23	24	25
26	27	28	29	30	31	

February

S	M	T	W	T	F	S
						1
2	3	4	5	6	7	8
9	10	11	12	13	14	15
16	17	18	19	20	21	22
23	24	25	26	27	28	29

March

S	M	T	W	T	F	S
1	2	3	4	5	6	7
8	9	10	11	12	13	14
15	16	17	18	19	20	21
22	23	24	25	26	27	28
29	30	31				

April

S	M	T	W	T	F	S
			1	2	3	4
5	6	7	8	9	10	11
12	13	14	15	16	17	18
19	20	21	22	23	24	25
26	27	28	29	30		

May

S	M	T	W	T	F	S
					1	2
3	4	5	6	7	8	9
10	11	12	13	14	15	16
17	18	19	20	21	22	23
24	25	26	27	28	29	30
31						

June

S	M	T	W	T	F	S
	1	2	3	4	5	6
7	8	9	10	11	12	13
14	15	16	17	18	19	20
21	22	23	24	25	26	27
28	29	30				

July

S	M	T	W	T	F	S
			1	2	3	4
5	6	7	8	9	10	11
12	13	14	15	16	17	18
19	20	21	22	23	24	25
26	27	28	29	30	31	

August

S	M	T	W	T	F	S
						1
2	3	4	5	6	7	8
9	10	11	12	13	14	15
16	17	18	19	20	21	22
23	24	25	26	27	28	29
30	31					

September

S	M	T	W	T	F	S
		1	2	3	4	5
6	7	8	9	10	11	12
13	14	15	16	17	18	19
20	21	22	23	24	25	26
27	28	29	30			

October

S	M	T	W	T	F	S
			1	2	3	4
5	6	7	8	9	10	11
12	13	14	15	16	17	18
19	20	21	22	23	24	25
26	27	28	29	30	31	

November

S	M	T	W	T	F	S
1	2	3	4	5	6	7
8	9	10	11	12	13	14
15	16	17	18	19	20	21
22	23	24	25	26	27	28
29	30					

December

S	M	T	W	T	F	S
		1	2	3	4	5
6	7	8	9	10	11	12
13	14	15	16	17	18	19
20	21	22	23	24	25	26
27	28	29	30	31		

Federal Holidays

Jan 1	New Year's Day	May 5	Cinco de Mayo	Nov 3	Election Day
Jan 20	Martin Luther King Jr. Day	May 10	Mother's Day	Nov 11	Veterans Day
Feb 14	Valentine's Day	May 25	Memorial Day	Nov 26	Thanksgiving Day
Feb 17	Presidents' Day (Most regions)	Jun 21	Father's Day	Nov 27	Black Friday
Mar 17	St. Patrick's Day	Jul 3	'Independence Day' observed	Dec 24	Christmas Eve
Apr 10	Good Friday (Many regions)	Jul 4	Independence Day	Dec 25	Christmas Day
Apr 12	Easter Sunday	Sep 7	Labor Day	Dec 31	New Year's Eve
Apr 13	Easter Monday	Oct 12	Columbus Day (Most regions)		
Apr 15	Tax Day	Oct 31	Halloween		

Date to Remember

January	February	March	April

May	June	July	August

September	October	November	December

01
JAN

December 2019
S	M	T	W	T	F	S
1	2	3	4	5	6	7
8	9	10	11	12	13	14
15	16	17	18	19	20	21
22	23	24	25	26	27	28
29	30	31				

SUNDAY	MONDAY	TUESDAY	WEDNESDAY
29	30	31	1 *New Year's Day*
5	6	7	8
12	13	14	15
19 36½ °C Just after tea	20 36½ °C *Martin Luther King Jr. Day*	21	22
26	27	28	29

February 2020

S M T W T F S
                1
2 3 4 5 6 7 8
9 10 11 12 13 14 15
16 17 18 19 20 21 22
23 24 25 26 27 28 29

2020

THURSDAY	FRIDAY	SATURDAY	NOTES
2	3	4	
9	10	11	
16	17 Temperature, 35°? 1700	18 36° 18,5	
23	24	25	
30	31	1	

02
FEB

January 2020
S	M	T	W	T	F	S
			1	2	3	4
5	6	7	8	9	10	11
12	13	14	15	16	17	18
19	20	21	22	23	24	25
26	27	28	29	30	31	

SUNDAY	MONDAY	TUESDAY	WEDNESDAY
26	27	28	29
2	3	4	5
9	10	11	12
16	17	18	19
	Presidents' Day		
23	24	25	26

March 2020

S	M	T	W	T	F	S
1	2	3	4	5	6	7
8	9	10	11	12	13	14
15	16	17	18	19	20	21
22	23	24	25	26	27	28
29	30	31				

2020

THURSDAY	FRIDAY	SATURDAY	NOTES
30	31	1	
6	7	8	
13	14 *Valentine's Day*	15	
20	21	22	
27	28	29	

03
MAR

February 2020
S	M	T	W	T	F	S
						1
2	3	4	5	6	7	8
9	10	11	12	13	14	15
16	17	18	19	20	21	22
23	24	25	26	27	28	29

SUNDAY	MONDAY	TUESDAY	WEDNESDAY
1	2	3	4
8	9	10	11
15	16	17 *St. Patrick's Day*	18
22	23	24	25
29	30	31	1

April 2020

S	M	T	W	T	F	S
			1	2	3	4
5	6	7	8	9	10	11
12	13	14	15	16	17	18
19	20	21	22	23	24	25
26	27	28	29	30		

2020

THURSDAY	FRIDAY	SATURDAY	NOTES
5	6	7	
12	13	14	
19	20	21	
26	27	28	
2	3	4	

04
APR

March 2020

S	M	T	W	T	F	S
1	2	3	4	5	6	7
8	9	10	11	12	13	14
15	16	17	18	19	20	21
22	23	24	25	26	27	28
29	30	31				

SUNDAY	MONDAY	TUESDAY	WEDNESDAY
29	30	31	1
5	6	7	8
12	13	14	15
Easter Sunday	*Easter Monday*		*Tax Day*
19	20	21	22
26	27	28	29

May 2020
S M T W T F S
            1 2
3 4 5 6 7 8 9
10 11 12 13 14 15 16
17 18 19 20 21 22 23
24 25 26 27 28 29 30
31

2020

THURSDAY	FRIDAY	SATURDAY	NOTES
2	3	4	
9	10 *Good Friday*	11	
16	17	18	
23	24	25	
30	1	2	

05
May

April 2020
S M T W T F S
1 2 3 4
5 6 7 8 9 10 11
12 13 14 15 16 17 18
19 20 21 22 23 24 25
26 27 28 29 30

SUNDAY	MONDAY	TUESDAY	WEDNESDAY
26	27	28	29
3	4	5 *Cinco de Mayo*	6
10 *Mother's Day*	11	12	13
17	18	19	20
24	25 *Memorial Day*	26	27
31	1	2	3

June 2020

S	M	T	W	T	F	S
	1	2	3	4	5	6
7	8	9	10	11	12	13
14	15	16	17	18	19	20
21	22	23	24	25	26	27
28	29	30				

2020

THURSDAY	FRIDAY	SATURDAY	NOTES
30	1	2	
7	8	9	
14	15	16	
21	22	23	
28	29	30	
4	5	6	

06
JUN

May 2020
S	M	T	W	T	F	S
					1	2
3	4	5	6	7	8	9
10	11	12	13	14	15	16
17	18	19	20	21	22	23
24	25	26	27	28	29	30
31						

SUNDAY	MONDAY	TUESDAY	WEDNESDAY
31	1	2	3
7	8	9	10
14	15	16	17
21 *Father's Day*	22	23	24
28	29	30	1

July 2020

S	M	T	W	T	F	S
			1	2	3	4
5	6	7	8	9	10	11
12	13	14	15	16	17	18
19	20	21	22	23	24	25
26	27	28	29	30	31	

2020

THURSDAY	FRIDAY	SATURDAY	NOTES
4	5	6	
11	12	13	
18	19	20	
25	26	27	
2	3	4	

07
Jul

June 2020
S	M	T	W	T	F	S
	1	2	3	4	5	6
7	8	9	10	11	12	13
14	15	16	17	18	19	20
21	22	23	24	25	26	27
28	29	30				

SUNDAY	MONDAY	TUESDAY	WEDNESDAY
28	29	30	1
5	6	7	8
12	13	14	15
19	20	21	22
26	27	28	29

August 2020

S	M	T	W	T	F	S
						1
2	3	4	5	6	7	8
9	10	11	12	13	14	15
16	17	18	19	20	21	22
23	24	25	26	27	28	29
30	31					

2020

THURSDAY	FRIDAY	SATURDAY	NOTES
2	3	4	
	'Independence Day' observed	*Independence Day*	
9	10	11	
16	17	18	
23	24	25	
30	31	1	

08
AUG

July 2020
S	M	T	W	T	F	S
			1	2	3	4
5	6	7	8	9	10	11
12	13	14	15	16	17	18
19	20	21	22	23	24	25
26	27	28	29	30	31	

SUNDAY	MONDAY	TUESDAY	WEDNESDAY
26	27	28	29
2	3	4	5
9	10	11	12
16	17	18	19
23	24	25	26
30	31	1	2

September 2020

S	M	T	W	T	F	S
		1	2	3	4	5
6	7	8	9	10	11	12
13	14	15	16	17	18	19
20	21	22	23	24	25	26
27	28	29	30			

2020

THURSDAY	FRIDAY	SATURDAY	NOTES
30	31	1	
6	7	8	
13	14	15	
20	21	22	
27	28	29	
3	4	5	

09
SEP

August 2020
S M T W T F S
1
2 3 4 5 6 7 8
9 10 11 12 13 14 15
16 17 18 19 20 21 22
23 24 25 26 27 28 29
30 31

SUNDAY	MONDAY	TUESDAY	WEDNESDAY
30	31	1	2
6	7 *Labor Day*	8	9
13	14	15	16
20	21	22	23
27	28	29	30

October 2020

S	M	T	W	T	F	S
				1	2	3
4	5	6	7	8	9	10
11	12	13	14	15	16	17
18	19	20	21	22	23	24
25	26	27	28	29	30	31

2020

THURSDAY	FRIDAY	SATURDAY	NOTES
3	4	5	
10	11	12	
17	18	19	
24	25	26	
1	2	3	

10
OCT

September 2020

S	M	T	W	T	F	S
		1	2	3	4	5
6	7	8	9	10	11	12
13	14	15	16	17	18	19
20	21	22	23	24	25	26
27	28	29	30			

SUNDAY	MONDAY	TUESDAY	WEDNESDAY
27	28	29	30
4	5	6	7
11	12 *Columbus Day*	13	14
18	19	20	21
25	26	27	28

November 2020

S	M	T	W	T	F	S
1	2	3	4	5	6	7
8	9	10	11	12	13	14
15	16	17	18	19	20	21
22	23	24	25	26	27	28
29	30					

2020

THURSDAY	FRIDAY	SATURDAY	NOTES
1	2	3	
8	9	10	
15	16	17	
22	23	24	
29	30	31 *Halloween*	

11
NOV

October 2020
S M T W T F S
          1 2 3
4 5 6 7 8 9 10
11 12 13 14 15 16 17
18 19 20 21 22 23 24
25 26 27 28 29 30 31

SUNDAY	MONDAY	TUESDAY	WEDNESDAY
1	2	3 *Election Day*	4
8	9	10	11 *Veterans Day*
15	16	17	18
22	23	24	25
29	30	1	2

December 2020

S	M	T	W	T	F	S
		1	2	3	4	5
6	7	8	9	10	11	12
13	14	15	16	17	18	19
20	21	22	23	24	25	26
27	28	29	30	31		

2020

THURSDAY	FRIDAY	SATURDAY	NOTES
5	6	7	
12	13	14	
19	20	21	
26 *Thanksgiving Day*	27 *Black Friday*	28	
3	4	5	

12
DEC

November 2020
S M T W T F S
1 2 3 4 5 6 7
8 9 10 11 12 13 14
15 16 17 18 19 20 21
22 23 24 25 26 27 28
29 30

SUNDAY	MONDAY	TUESDAY	WEDNESDAY
29	30	1	2
6	7	8	9
13	14	15	16
20	21	22	23
27	28	29	30

January 2021

S	M	T	W	T	F	S
					1	2
3	4	5	6	7	8	9
10	11	12	13	14	15	16
17	18	19	20	21	22	23
24	25	26	27	28	29	30
31						

2020

THURSDAY	FRIDAY	SATURDAY	NOTES
3	4	5	
10	11	12	
17	18	19	
24	25	26	
Christmas Eve	*Christmas Day*		
31	1	2	
New Year's Eve			

1 | Wednesday
January

3 | Friday
January

5

Sunday
January

7 Tuesday
January

9

Thursday
January

11 | Saturday
January

13 | Monday
January

Tuesday
January

14

15 | Wednesday
January

17 | Friday
January

RETURNED HOME FROM
HOSPITAL. MAMA BEAR DROVE US
HOME VIA BLAGDON HILL
SO WONDERFUL TO SEE SKY + CLOUDS
AND TREES + FIELDS AND VIEWS
FROM THE TOP OF THE HILL
CALLED IN AT BARLEYMOWS FOR
FLOWERS - HOME - UNBELIEVABLE
TO BE HOME AT LAST - PEACEFUL
AND QUIET AFTER THE NOISE
AND LACK OF SLEEP + MENTAL
CRUSHING OF MPH

Saturday
January | **18**

WEATHER BRIGHT + FROSTY

MESSAGES FROM SUZANNE
AND HELENA. DEAR FRIENDS
LOVELY PHONE CALL FROM ANDREW
TRIED TO BE SUPPORTIVE OF HIS SITUATION
GOAL   RE MOTHERS WILL ETC

TO WALK ALL ALONG THE
SEA FRONT AT SEATON TO THE
HIDEAWAY CAFE. HAVE LOVELY
FOOD + DRINK THERE AND THEN
RETURN TO THE CAR AT THE OTHER END
OF THE SEA FRONT.

NOT A VERY GOOD NIGHT -
3-5 OR 4 HOURS SLEEP.
COLD NIGHT - BACK HURTING
TRIED SLEEPING WITH LIGHT
OFF - NO NIGHTMARES SO FAR

INTO OUR BED ♒ 7:15 AM
BACK STILL HURT. THINGS GOT
BETTER ONCE I HAD CLEAN JAMA
TOP + BOTTOMS ON PLUS DRESSING
GOWN - IN BED / GOT INTO A COMFY
POSITION, STARTED TO WARM UP.
LOVELY TEA IN BED. BRIGHT FROSTY
MORNING - AMAZING 'CLAIRLIE' SLY
DOWNSTAIRS TO SIT IN CARVER CHAIR
WITH RUGS, LEG WARMERS ON + BOOS
GETTING COMFORTABLE. LOOKING
FORWARD TO PORRIDGE - YUMM!

21 | Tuesday
January

23 | Thursday
January

25 Saturday
January

Sunday
January | **26**

27 | Monday
January

29 | **Wednesday**
January

31 | Friday
January

Saturday
February | 1

2 Sunday
February

Monday
February | **3**

FEB

4

Tuesday
February

6 Thursday
February

8 Saturday
February

10 | Monday
February

12 | Wednesday
February

Thursday
February | 13

14 | Friday
February

16 Sunday
February

FEB

18 | Tuesday
February

FEB

22 Saturday
February

24 Monday
February

26 Wednesday
February

FEB

28 | Friday
February

1

Sunday
March

3

Tuesday
March

5

Thursday
March

7

Saturday
March

Sunday
March

8

MAR

9

Monday
March

MAR

11 | Wednesday
March

13 | Friday
March

15 Sunday
March

17 | Tuesday
March

19 | Thursday
March

21 Saturday
March

23 | Monday
March

25 | Wednesday
March

27

Friday
March

Saturday
March 28

MAR

29

Sunday
March

MAR

Monday
March
30

31

Tuesday
March

2 | Thursday
April

4 | Saturday
April

Sunday
April | 5

6 | Monday
April

APR

8

Wednesday
April

10 | Friday
April

12 Sunday
April

14 Tuesday
April

16 Thursday
April

18 Saturday
April

20 | Monday
April

Tuesday
April | **21**

APR

22 | **Wednesday**
April

APR

24 | Friday
April

Saturday
April | **25**

APR

26

Sunday
April

28

Tuesday
April

30

Thursday
April

2 | Saturday
May

4 | Monday
May

MAY

6 | Wednesday
May

8

Friday
May

Saturday
May | 9

MAY

10 | Sunday
May

12 | Tuesday
May

Wednesday
May
13

MAY

14 | Thursday
May

16 | Saturday
May

18 | Monday
May

20 Wednesday
May

22 | Friday
May

24 Sunday
May

26 Tuesday
May

Wednesday
May | **27**

MAY

28 Thursday
May

30

Saturday
May

1 | Monday
June

Tuesday
June | 2

JUN

3 | Wednesday
June

JUN

5

Friday
June

JUN

Saturday
June | 6

7 | Sunday
June

9

Tuesday
June

11 Thursday
June

13 | Saturday
June

Sunday
June | 14

15 | Monday
June

17 | Wednesday
June

19 | Friday
June

21 Sunday
June

JUN

23 Tuesday
June

25 | Thursday
June

JUN

27 Saturday
June

29 | Monday
June

1

Wednesday
July

3 | Friday
July

5 | Sunday
July

7

Tuesday
July

9 | Thursday
July

11 | Saturday
July

13 | Monday
July

15 | Wednesday
July

17 | Friday
July

19 Sunday
July

21 | Tuesday
July

23 | Thursday
July

25 | Saturday
July

27 | Monday
July

Tuesday
July 28

JUL

29 | Wednesday
July

JUL

31

Friday
July

JUL

2 | Sunday
August

Monday
August

3

4 Tuesday
August

6 | Thursday
August

8 Saturday
August

10 Monday
August

Tuesday
August | 11

12 Wednesday
August

Thursday
August
13

14 | Friday
August

16 | Sunday
August

18 | Tuesday
August

AUG

20 | Thursday
August

22 | Saturday
August

24 | Monday
August

AUG

26 Wednesday
August

28 | Friday
August

30 Sunday
August

1

Tuesday
September

3 | Thursday
September

Friday
September | 4

5 Saturday
September

Sunday
September
6

7 | Monday
September

Tuesday
September

8

9 | **Wednesday**
September

11 | Friday
September

13

Sunday
September

15

Tuesday
September

17 | Thursday
September

19 | Saturday
September

21 | Monday
September

Tuesday
September | **22**

SEP

23 | Wednesday
September

Thursday
September | **24**

SEP

25 | Friday
September

27

Sunday
September

29 | Tuesday
September

1

Thursday
October

3

Saturday
October

OCT

5 Monday
October

Tuesday
October

6

7

Wednesday
October

9

Friday
October

Saturday | 10
October

OCT

11 Sunday
October

13 Tuesday
October

15 | **Thursday**
October

17 Saturday
October

19 | Monday
October

21 | Wednesday
October

Thursday | 22
October

OCT

23 | Friday
October

25 | Sunday
October

OCT

27 | Tuesday
October

29 Thursday
October

31

Saturday
October

2 | Monday
November

4

Wednesday
November

6 Friday
November

Saturday
November | **7**

NOV

8 Sunday
November

Monday
November

9

NOV

10 | Tuesday
November

12 | Thursday
November

Friday
November | 13

NOV

14 Saturday
November

16 | Monday
November

18 | Wednesday
November

20 Friday
November

22 | Sunday
November

24 | Tuesday
November

NOV

26 Thursday
November

28 Saturday
November

30

Monday
November

2

Wednesday
December

Thursday
December

3

4

Friday
December

Saturday
December | **5**

DEC

6 Sunday
December

8 Tuesday
December

10 | Thursday
December

12 | Saturday
December

14 Monday
December

16 | Wednesday
December

Thursday
December | **17**

18 | Friday
December

20 | Sunday
December

22 | Tuesday
December

24 | Thursday
December

26 Saturday
December

28 | Monday
December

30 Wednesday
December

Thursday
December | **31**

Printed in Poland
by Amazon Fulfillment
Poland Sp. z o.o., Wrocław

52662246R00222